Lexile: _____

AR/BL: _____2.8_____

AR Points: ___0.5_____

DK READERS

Level 1

A Day at Greenhill Farm
Truck Trouble
Tale of a Tadpole
Surprise Puppy!
Duckling Days
A Day at Seagull Beach
Whatever the Weather
Busy Buzzy Bee
Big Machines
Wild Baby Animals
A Bed for the Winter
Born to be a Butterfly
Dinosaur's Day
Feeding Time
Diving Dolphin
Rockets and Spaceships
My Cat's Secret
First Day at Gymnastics
A Trip to the Zoo
I Can Swim!
A Trip to the Library
A Trip to the Doctor
A Trip to the Dentist
I Want to be a Ballerina
Animal Hide and Seek
Submarines and Submersibles
Animals at Home
Let's Play Soccer

Homes Around the World
LEGO: Trouble at the Bridge
LEGO: Secret at Dolphin Bay
Star Wars: What is a Wookie?
Star Wars: Ready, Set, Podrace!
Star Wars: Luke Skywalker's Amazing
   Story
Star Wars: Tatooine Adventures
Star Wars The Clone Wars: Watch Out for
   Jabba the Hutt!
Star Wars The Clone Wars: Pirates... and
   Worse
Power Rangers: Jungle Fury: We are the
   Power Rangers
LEGO Duplo: Around Town
LEGO Pirates: Brickbeard's Treasure
Indiana Jones: Indy's Adventures
John Deere: Good Morning, Farm!
A Day in the Life of a Builder
A Day in the Life of a Dancer
A Day in the Life of a Firefighter
A Day in the Life of a Teacher
A Day in the Life of a Musician
A Day in the Life of a Doctor
A Day in the Life of a Police Officer
A Day in the Life of a TV Reporter
Gigantes de Hierro *en español*
Crías del mundo animal *en español*

Level 2

Crías del mundo animal en español
Dinosaur Dinners
Fire Fighter!
Bugs! Bugs! Bugs!
Slinky, Scaly Snakes!
Animal Hospital
The Little Ballerina
Munching, Crunching, Sniffing, and
   Snooping
The Secret Life of Trees
Winking, Blinking, Wiggling, and
   Waggling
Astronaut: Living in Space
Twisters!
Holiday! Celebration Days around the
   World
The Story of Pocahontas
Horse Show
Survivors: The Night the Titanic Sank
Eruption! The Story of Volcanoes
The Story of Columbus
Journey of a Humpback Whale
Amazing Buildings
Feathers, Flippers, and Feet
Outback Adventure: Australian Vacation
Sniffles, Sneezes, Hiccups, and Coughs
Ice Skating Stars
Let's Go Riding
I Want to Be a Gymnast

Starry Sky
Earth Smart: How to Take Care
   of the Environment
Water Everywhere
Telling Time
A Trip to the Theater
Journey of a Pioneer
Inauguration Day
Star Wars: Journey Through Space
Star Wars: A Queen's Diary
Star Wars: R2-D2 and Friends
Star Wars: Jedi in Training
Star Wars: Join the Rebels
Star Wars: Clone Troopers in Action
Star Wars: The Clone Wars: Anakin in
   Action!
Star Wars: The Clone Wars: Stand Aside
   – Bounty Hunters!
WWE: John Cena
Spider-Man: Worst Enemies
Power Rangers: Great Adventures
Pokémon: Meet the Pokémon
Pokémon: Meet Ash!
LEGO Kingdoms: Defend the Castle
Meet the X-Men
Indiana Jones: Traps and Snares
¡Insectos! en español
¡Bomberos! en español
La Historia de Pocahontas en español

A Note to Parents

DK READERS is a compelling program for beginning readers, designed in conjunction with leading literacy experts, including Dr. Linda Gambrell, Professor of Education at Clemson University. Dr. Gambrell has served as President of the National Reading Conference and the College Reading Association, and has recently been elected to serve as President of the International Reading Association.

Beautiful illustrations and superb full-color photographs combine with engaging, easy-to-read stories to offer a fresh approach to each subject in the series. Each DK READER is guaranteed to capture a child's interest while developing his or her reading skills, general knowledge, and love of reading.

The five levels of DK READERS are aimed at different reading abilities, enabling you to choose the books that are exactly right for your child:

Pre-level 1: Learning to read
Level 1: Beginning to read
Level 2: Beginning to read alone
Level 3: Reading alone
Level 4: Proficient readers

The "normal" age at which a child begins to read can be anywhere from three to eight years old. Adult participation through the lower levels is very helpful for providing encouragement, discussing storylines, and sounding out unfamiliar words.

No matter which level you select, you can be sure that you are helping your child learn to read, then read to learn!

LONDON, NEW YORK, MUNICH,
MELBOURNE, AND DELHI

Editor Hannah Dolan
Designer Rhys Thomas
Senior Designer Rob Perry
Managing Art Editor Ron Stobbart
Art Director Lisa Lanzarini
Publishing Manager Catherine Saunders
Associate Publisher Simon Beecroft
Category Publisher Alex Allan
Production Editor Clare McLean
Production Controller Nick Seston

Reading Consultant
Linda B. Gambrell, Ph.D.

First published in the United States in 2011
by DK Publishing
375 Hudson Street, New York, New York 10014

11 12 13 14 15 10 9 8 7 6 5 4 3 2 1

176218—12/10

DK books are available at special discounts when purchased in bulk
for sales promotions, premiums, fund-raising, or educational use.
For details, contact:
DK Publishing Special Markets
375 Hudson Street
New York, New York 10014
SpecialSales@dk.com

A catalog record for this book is available
from the Library of Congress.

ISBN: 978-0-7566-7706-0 (Paperback)
ISBN: 978-0-7566-7707-7 (Hardcover)

Color reproduction by MDP
Printed and bound in China by L-Rex

Discover more at
www.dk.com

www.LEGO.com

DK READERS

BEGINNING TO READ 1

LEGO PIRATES

Brickbeard's Treasure

Written by Hannah Dolan

DK

Ahoy, me hearty!
That means "Hello, my friend!"
to a pirate.
This fierce pirate is called
Captain Brickbeard.

He is the captain of this ship.
It is called *Brickbeard's Bounty*.

Captain Brickbeard
and his crew sail
the high seas in
Brickbeard's Bounty.

treasure

They are always looking for treasure and adventure. Let's go aboard the ship and have a look around!

Look at the top of the ship
and you will see a black flag.

flag

The flag has a skull
and some bones on it.
It is called the Jolly Roger.
It will scare the pirates'
enemies away!

Can you see the pretty mermaid on the ship? She is called a figurehead. The pirates hope that she will bring the ship good luck in stormy seas and shark-filled waters!

figurehead

The ship has powerful cannons.
The pirates use them when they
do battle with their enemies.
The pirates' enemies are other
treasure-seekers on the high seas!

The soldiers of the King's Navy protect the high seas from pirates. They are always looking for pirates who are up to no good!

The King's soldiers are the pirates'
biggest enemies.

Sometimes the King's soldiers take
the pirates' treasure.

Sometimes the pirates steal theirs!

What's this? One of the pirates
has found an old treasure map!
The cross on it tells him where
treasure is buried.

This soldier wants the map, too.

Look out!

He is firing cannon balls
with his big cannon!

An old pirate is guarding
treasure on this island.
His pirate ship left
him behind!

The pirates and the King's
soldiers have found the
treasure!
Who will
reach it first?

These pirates have some treasure!
They are on a wooden raft.
The raft floats along very slowly.
The pirates are taking their
treasure to *Brickbeard's Bounty*.

raft

This sea monster is another enemy of the pirates!
It loves shiny treasure, too.
It has eight arms to help it steal the pirates' treasure!

The pirates must keep
their treasure safe.
They hide it in their
secret hideout.
It has hidden
traps to scare
away enemies!

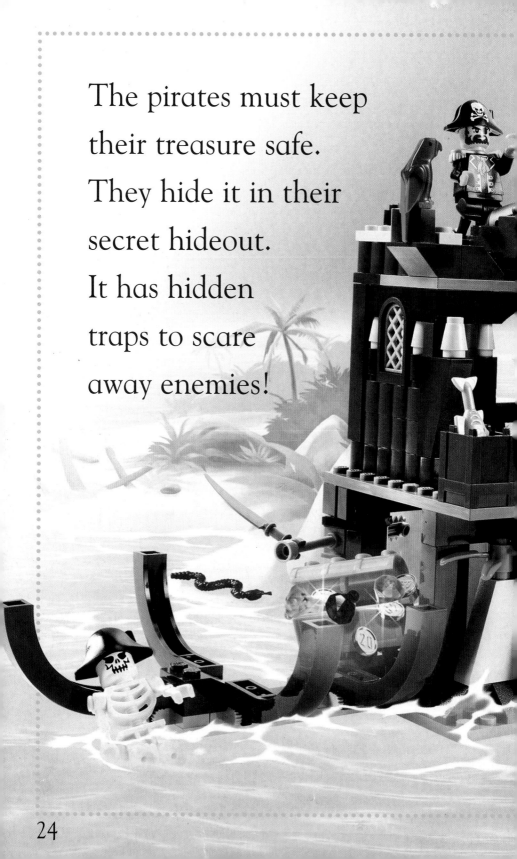

Look out, pirates!
These soldiers
have found your hideout!

This is the King's Navy's fortress.
It is where the King's soldiers
keep their treasure safe.

fortress

Look! Captain Brickbeard wants
to steal the soldiers' treasure!

The fortress has a prison cell.
The soldiers have locked up a
pirate in the prison cell.
Look who is here to rescue him!

prison cell

Captain Brickbeard's clever pet
monkey is trained to steal things.
He steals the key to the prison
cell and sets the pirate free!

Now you know all about
pirates, you could be one too.
You can enjoy your own
pirate adventures!

"Goodbye, me hearty," says Captain Brickbeard.

Glossary

page 6

treasure

page 8

flag

page 10

figurehead

page 20

raft

page 26

fortress

page 28

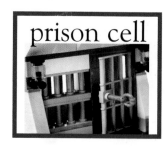

prison cell

Index